Contents

Dedications: 2
Tags & Legend 3
Unclog the Drain - Workbook 15
   Questions 15
   Practical Exercise: 30

Dedications:

Thank you, to my Lord and Savior; for giving me the desire and skill-set to accomplish something to help guide others.

Thank you to my Wife, (Crystal Danyel); for the love, patience, and understanding while I spent a great amount of time and effort developing the content of this project.

Thank you to the people and organization's whom imparted financial literacy and empowerment into me before it was too late to recover.

Thank you to Lincoln & Hill; for seeing this project as a viable asset to the mission & vision.

Tags & Legend

 Divide-Digital Tag: depicts the differences perceived by access to or lack of global information

 Ex Tag: depicts a person, a place or thing from your past

 Household Tag: depicts a situation that should be handled within the home

 Lighthouse Tag: depicts being a valid example within God's will

 Gateway Tag: depicts sensory messages (subliminally or consciously) to influence the decisions of a targeted demographic

 Big Brother Tag: depicts someone is always surveilling the masses

 Microscope Tag: depicts extreme observation will take place as a result of past or present actions

Social Issue Tag: depicts issues centered around injustices of a particular demographic

 Back against the wall Tag: depicts unfavorable circumstances; past, present, and foreseeable future

 Booking Tag: depicts an opportunity for a speaker is available

Caveat Tag: depicts a specific threat when considering additional information about this subject

Coach Tag: depicts a personal philosophy is available to be learned

Commentary Tag: depicts supplementary data through public research & discussions that we may oppose or support but use for teaching purposes

Content tag: depicts supplementary data through public research & discussions that we may oppose or support but use for teaching

 Cornerstone Principle Tag: depicts a fundamental principle

 Directional Tag: depicts perceived versus true direction of moral compass

 Discipleship Tag: depicts lesson that require a mentor/mentee relationship

 Divide-Cultural Tag: depicts the differences perceived by ethnicity

 Divide-Economical Tag: depicts the differences perceived by financial assets and net-worth

 Divide-Educational Tag: depicts the differences perceived by access to and completion of higher education

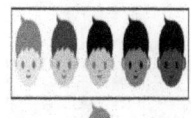 Divide-Racial Tag: depicts the differences perceived by outer physical appearance

 End-of-Rope Tag: depicts the end of human strength and the beginning of God's strength

 Entertainment-Private Tag: depicts social enactments inside the dwelling

 Evangelism Tag: depicts the opportunity to spread the good news

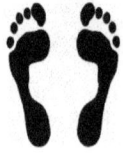 Film Tag: depicts supplementary data through developed footage to support or refute a philosophy or teaching

 Footsteps Ordered Tag: depicts a path inspired by faith in God's will

 Forces-Unseen Tag: depicts intangible spiritual opposition

 Gender-Female Tag: depicts the actions of a female has transpired

 Gender-Male Tag: depicts the actions of a male has transpired

 Gender-Man Tag: depicts the actions of a man is required

 Gender-Woman Tag: depicts the actions of a woman is required

Healing Tag: depicts a person, a place or thing that can help start the healing process.

 Hearing the Word Tag: depicts the individually or corporately heard proclamations of the scriptures

 In-a-Hole Tag: depicts a previous choice that has put a person or people in an immoral situation or at a disadvantage

 Influenced Tag: depicts the people, places or things that individuals get swayed by

 Influencer Tag: depicts the people, places or things that sway other individuals

 Inner Struggle Tag: depicts opposing options are available but only one can be selected

 Issue-Educational Tag: depicts an issue pertaining to the education system

 Read It Tag: depicts a lesson or information that requires reading

LIFE project Tag: depicts principles associated with the training curricula

 Measured Tag: depicts the qualitative or quantitative results of circumstances portrayed or observed

Motivational Tag: depicts more energy is needed to prevail in current circumstances

Nugget Tag: depicts more information can be learned about a person, a place or thing with a desire to dig deeper

Parental Tag: depicts a decision must be made with the best interest of the child/children at its core

Pause Tag: depicts taking a break within a situation to rethink direction before proceeding

Pivot Point Tag: depicts a juncture that the movement required, changes the trajectory permanently

Plan Tag: depicts individuals or a couple have written procedures to follow

 Positive/Negative Tag: depicts the current situation has a 50/50 potential of going either direction

 Prayer Tag: depicts the need for the power of prayer is imminent

 Replay Tag: depicts the attempt to retry a circumstance from the past to accomplish a different outcome without new skills or information

 Rewind Tag: depicts the attempt to review the past to reflect on mistakes

 Risk Tag: depicts incorrectly placing faith in chance

 Skip Tag: depicts the attempt to bypass steps in the process

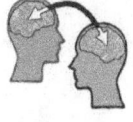 Temptation Tag: depicts a person, a place or things that is a potential hindrance to an objective

Testimony Tag: depicts a former test that requires sharing of a testament of survival

Transferred Knowledge Tag: depicts information shared with the next generation

Under the Radar Tag: depicts a subject that is going unnoticed purposely or unintentionally

Video Tag: depicts supplementary data through digital footage to support or refute a philosophy or teaching

 Watchman Tag: depicts a person/mentee could be observing how you behave or respond

Action Time Tag: depicts individuals or a couple must physically move on principle learned

Active Listening Tag: depicts one individual should be actively listening each time another individual is talking in the communication process

 Advice Tag: depicts information from confidant for emphasizing key point

 Caution Tag: depicts the subject or information should be approached carefully

 Challenge Tag: depicts individuals or a couple must complete an assignment immediately before moving to next concept

Championed Tag: depicts a social philosophy that is influencing others positively or negatively

Checkpoint Tag: depicts a location gauge during subject or individual progression

 Communicate Tag: depicts general subject matter verbalized between male & female cohorts

Connection Tag: depicts a link to other materials available through the L.I.F.E project

Discussion Tag: depicts specific subject matter verbalized between male & female cohorts

 Divide-Political Tag: depicts the differences perceived by political affiliation

 Entertainment-Public Tag: depicts social enactments outside the dwelling

 Fast Forward Tag: depicts visualization of the future direction of individuals dictated by actions taken

Woo Tag: depicts attempting to physically or mentally influence an individual temporarily

Forces-Seen Tag: depicts tangible human opposition

Go back Tag: depicts individuals or a couple is required to review a subject already mentioned

High Priority Tag: depicts critical information or concept in specific session or chapters about a particular subject

Investigate Tag: depicts individuals or a couple should further research & study subject matter

 Issue-Financial Tag: depicts an issue pertaining to the economic system

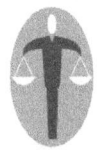 Issue-Judicial Tag: depicts an issue pertaining the justice system

 Issue-Political Tag: depicts an issue pertaining to the political process

 Works Tag: depicts something that can be done through individual effort

 Key Point Tag: depicts main topics covered in specific subject, session or chapter

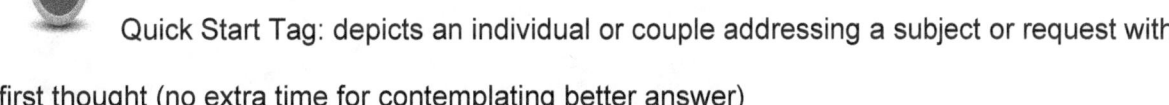 Practical Exercise Tag: depicts individuals or a couple must complete an assignment before next session can proceed

Quick Start Tag: depicts an individual or couple addressing a subject or request with first thought (no extra time for contemplating better answer)

Reflection Tag: depicts individuals thinking about subject or questions before providing an answer

Sand of Time Tag: depicts individuals or a couple must make a time sensitive decision to proceed

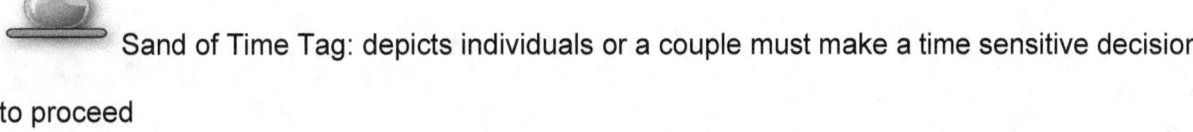 Beyond The Box Tag: depicts behaviors, thoughts, actions outside normal scope of individuals or group

 Change Tag: depicts a personal evolution that is forces or natural

Life Hack Tag: depicts a strategy or technique adopted to manage time and activities more efficiently

Opportunity Tag: depicts a potential opportunity is present but not commonly taken by those unprepared to seize it

Unclog the Drain - Workbook

The questions below reflect some of the most common areas related to any of the Unclog the Drain sessions. Answer all questions. **Discuss & Share** your answers with your cohort to provide understanding for each of your responses. Make additional notes if questions/concern aren't answered immediately, information provided in all sessions will help you get clarification plus provide informational cross-referencing.

Questions

 (Economical Divide Tag)

1. In your opinion, what are some effects of an economically divided community, nation or globe? Be specific

(Inner Struggle Tag)

1. What principles of economics creates the most personal conflict for you?

(Caveat Tag)

1. Many take unrealistic chances, how much significance do you put towards "your ship coming in" aside from working your financial plan? Be specific

(Watchman Tag)

1. Are there any young people (family or non-family) that are closely following how you earn money, spend money or manage money? If so, what are you showing them? Be specific

(Temptation Tag)

1. What makes you indulge in spending when you should be saving or investing? Why?

(End of Rope Tag)

1. When you have reached the end of your financial knowledge, experience or understanding; what steps do you take next? Why? Where did you learn those steps if any?

(Political Divide Tag)

1. What does the concept, "voting with your money" mean to you? Explain your answer

[ ]

(In A Hole Tag)

1. Many families speak of "curses", what attributes of your family or neighborhood have you allegedly been cursed with financially? Be specific, if none substitute other jinxes or superstitions you have lived by concerning money

[ ]

(Pivot Point Tag)

1. If you have experienced a major financial change (pivot) in your life, what caused it and why? Be specific

[ ]

(Change Tag)

1. What money savvy, money management, money exchange, money planning, money structure or money investment have you not be doing or have gotten away from, that you would like to return too or incorporate? Why?

(Advice Tag)

1. What's in the best financial empowerment advice you have received thus far? Explain your answer and who it came from?

(Household Tag)

1. Is the household you preside over/in, on one accord concerning economics or a budget plan? If not, what are the different approaches and how does it affect continuity?

(Life Hack Tag)

1. What are you doing to shift from linear earning to residual earning? If not doing so, do you have a plan for retirement? Be specific

(Public Entertainment Tag)

1. Within an instant gratification society, the entertainment industry is making trillions of dollars providing services, what is guiding your financial thoughts, decisions, and actions based on the entertainment you desire? Be specific

(Big Brother Tag)

1. What is your opinion about the government having laws concerning money transfers or deposit limits? Be specific

🔑 (Key Points Tag)

1. It is taboo to talk about money or compensation at work (corporate America), are you willing to share what you make with others to prevent from being underpaid?

[   ]

🌐 (Discussion Tag)

1. As a money earner (tax payer), with whom do you communicate about finances? Explain your answer

[   ]

⌛ (Sands of Time Tag)

1. Are you letting society, the media, and other external influencers dictate or sabotage your financial behavior or interactions? Are you coerced into rash purchase decisions?

[   ]

🎓 (Educational Divide Tag)

1. Do you believe your current educational status, is effecting your financial empowerment status? If so, what would make you change your status? If not, what keeps you from being effected?

🧰 (Works Tag)

1. Most people who have worked a job, have heard or lived "an honest pay for an honest day's work", what determines the amount of an honest day's work? Are you being compensated appropriately? Be specific

🎲 (Risk Tag)

1. Are you willing to risk your reputation (to go without) materials things the masses obtain? Do you believe this behavior of "keeping up with the Jones's" is acceptable? (please, not just a yes or no answer) Explain your answer

🔲 (Measured Tag)

1. What is your belief (measurement) of successful as it relates to finances? Explain your answers (we presuppose your definition of success is a reasonable one)

👪 (Parental Tag)

1. If you're a parent, are you custodial, non-custodial or other? Depending on your response, what are the financial ramification surrounding the raising of your child or children? Be specific. If you have no children, what is your approach to being finically stable to support a family? Explain your answers

✊ (Social Issue Tag)

1. Where do you stand as a money earner on boycotting big business or supporting small community businesses for social change? Do your social views negatively affect your profession, family or community status?

(Transfer Knowledge Tag)

1. Do you feel equipped to share financial information or lessons to other people?

(Influencer Tag)

1. In every stage of life, each person has someone that can sway them (good or bad); who is financially influencing you currently (it could be a brand or person)? Why?

(Directional Tag)

1. As a person, where is your financial compass taking your life? If not aware of your direction, where would you like to be headed…if you started a financial plan today?

⏸ (Pause Tag)

1. Have you ever taken a moment to (pause, breath, think) about the opportunity cost surrounding the "living for the weekend" mentality? If so, does it help you? If not, are your responses to spending money mostly emotional outburst? Explain your answer.

💬 (Positive-Negative Tag)

1. Do you ride the fence between being broke or living paycheck-to-paycheck while being a social media "balla"? If yes, explain the thinking behind having this mentality. If no, explain the mind frame that keeps you away from this mentality.

👤 (Coach Tag)

1. Has someone (colleague, friend, or family member) been trying to teach you something about economics or money management that you have refused to accept (intentionally or unintentionally)? If so, why have you refused the lesson? If not, do you wish to have a financial mentor? Be specific

(Planning Tag)

1. What is your financial plan? Is it written down? If so, who else knows about it? If not, what is keeping you from having a plan?

| |
| |

(Content Tag)

1. What information (books, podcast, television, social media etc.) are you feeding your thoughts and concerns related to financial empowerment, equity, and economics with? What effect does it have on your money decisions? Be specific

| |
| |

(Investigate Tag)

1. As an individual, is there any associations between laws, politics, and social injustice; you should examine deeper before moving forward with an economic decision? Explain your answer

| |
| |

(Under the Radar Tag)

1. With the changing laws of taxes and tax breaks; is the suspected attack on the lower income individuals/families, creating hidden preconceptions, thoughts, or agendas for you? If so, are you able to communicate what they are? If not, would you communicate about these issue publically?

(Championed Tag)

1. With the increased acceptance of "getting money" by unscrupulous or illegal means, what is your beliefs concerning the effect of recycling illicit (dirty) money in the community? Explain your answer

(Beyond The Box Tag)

1. Are you comfortable using the information you've been introduced to, in order to keep yourself from being stifled economically by society? Explain your answer

🧎 (Prayer Tag)

1. Many lower income, or financial stifled people pray for financial breakthroughs, if prayer is your primary means of gaining sounds principles concerning stewardship, what are your alternative means of gaining financial knowledge? Be specific

(Gateway Tag)

1. With subliminal sensory messages flooding all media platforms, what are your thoughts concerning economics and the power it seemingly yields? Where and on what do you spend your money? Do you believe, there is hidden messages that the masses might be overlooking in advertising?

(Discipleship Tag)

1. Who are your successor(s) and what are you teaching them about financial empowerment? If none, what circumstances have prevented from you beginning to train someone? Explain your answers

(Cornerstone Principle Tag)

1. Do you have a fundamental stance about financial empowerment? Will you forgo it? If so, why? If not, what is the standard behind your belief?

(Back Against the Wall Tag)

1. When you're up against the consequences of life's difficulties; what financial emergency plan do you utilize? If none, why not? How do you get immediate breathing room, when you're financial strapped? Be specific

(Nugget Tag)

1. What concept within money management have you been intrigued to dig deeper into its meaning, to better equip yourself? Explain your answer

🔬 (Microscope Tag)

1. Once you begin to change toward being smart with money matters, more family and friends will seek you out for loans, gifts, and investment opportunities. Do you have a strategic plan for each type of request?

💡 (Opportunity Tag)

1. As you become smarter in money matters, opportunities will also present themselves accordingly. Do you know how to research, compare or pursue valid opportunities? Are you willing to learn about investments?

Unclog the Drain| Clearing the Pipeline to Economic Empowerment

Practical Exercise:

 *Practical Exercise*

Of the four (4) categories; as a learning money manager, where do you put your money respectively? How much and why is this amount important? Be specific

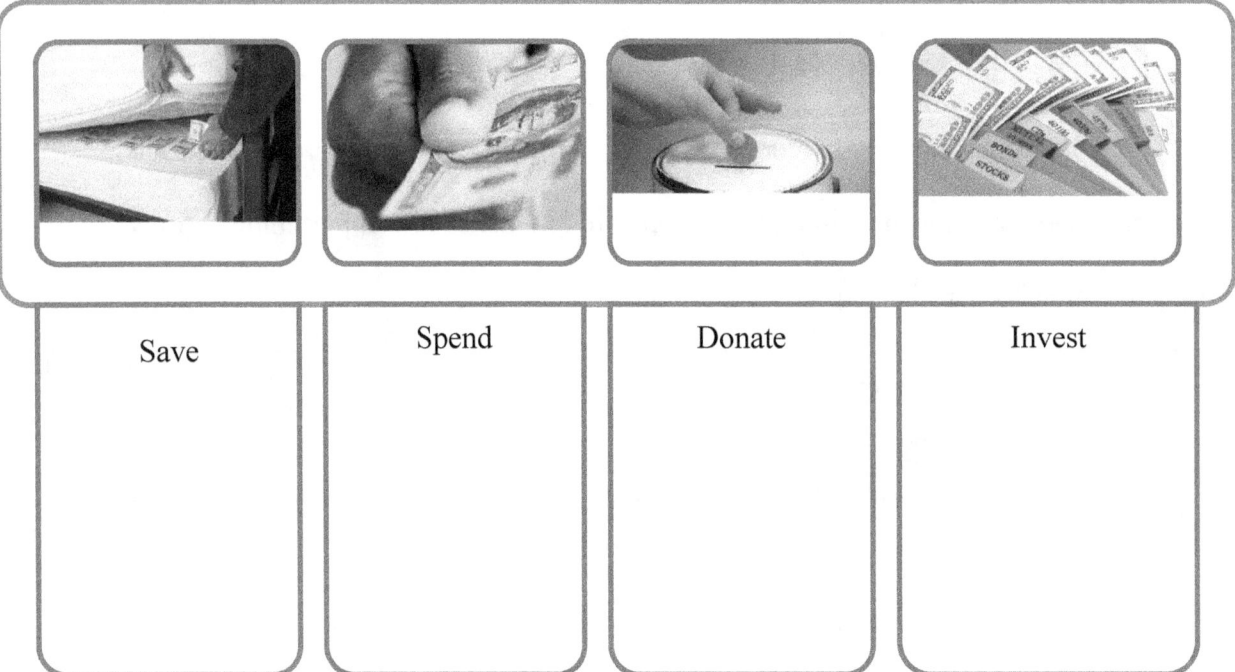

Save	Spend	Donate	Invest

www.ingramcontent.com/pod-product-compliance
Lightning Source LLC
Chambersburg PA
CBHW080531190526
45169CB00008B/3119